HOLY RULE OF SAINT BENEDICT

BENEDICT OF NURSIA

Translated by
BONIFACE VERHEYEN

CONTENTS

Prologue	1
1. Of the Kinds or the Life of Monks	5
2. What Kind of Man the Abbot Ought to Be	7
3. Of Calling the Brethren for Counsel	11
4. The Instruments of Good Works	13
5. Of Obedience	17
6. Of Silence	19
7. Of Humility	21
8. Of the Divine Office during the Night	27
9. How Many Psalms Are to Be Said at the Night Office	28
10. How the Office Is to Be Said during the Summer Season	30
11. How the Night Office Is to Be Said on Sundays	31
12. How Lauds Are to Be Said	33
13. How Lauds Are to Be Said on Week Days	34
14. How the Night Office Is to Be Said on the Feasts of the Saints	36
15. At What Times the Alleluia Is to Be Said	37
16. How the Work of God Is to Be Performed during the Day	38
17. How Many Psalms Are to Be Sung at These Hours	39
18. In What Order the Psalms Are to Be Said	41
19. Of the Manner of Reciting the Psalter	44
20. Of Reverence at Prayer	45
21. Of the Deans of the Monastery	46
22. How the Monks Are to Sleep	47
23. Of Excommunication for Faults	48
24. What the Manner of Excommunication Should Be	49
25. Of Graver Faults	50
26. Of Those Who without the Command of the Abbot Associate with the Excommunicated	51

27. How Concerned the Abbot Should Be about the Excommunicated	52
28. Of Those Who Having Often Been Corrected Do Not Amend	54
29. Whether Brethren Who Leave the Monastery Ought to Be Received Again	56
30. How Young Boys Are to Be Corrected	57
31. The Kind of Man the Cellarer of the Monastery Ought to Be	58
32. Of the Tools and Goods of the Monastery	60
33. Whether Monks Ought to Have Anything of Their Own	61
34. Whether All Should Receive in Equal Measure What Is Necessary	62
35. Of the Weekly Servers in the Kitchen	63
36. Of the Sick Brethren	65
37. Of the Aged and Children	67
38. Of the Weekly Reader	68
39. Of the Quantity of Food	70
40. Of the Quantity of Drink	72
41. At What Times the Brethren Should Take Their Refection	74
42. That No One Speak after Complin	76
43. Of Those Who Are Tardy in Coming to the Work of God or to Table	78
44. Of Those Who Are Excommunicated—How They Make Satisfaction	80
45. Of Those Who Commit a Fault in the Oratory	82
46. Of Those Who Fail in Any Other Matters	83
47. Of Giving the Signal for the Time of the Work of God	84
48. Of the Daily Work	85
49. On the Keeping of Lent	88
50. Of Brethren Who Work a Long Distance from the Oratory or Are on a Journey	90
51. Of the Brethren Who Do Not Go Very Far Away	91
52. Of the Oratory of the Monastery	92
53. Of the Reception of Guests	93

54. Whether a Monk Should Receive Letters or Anything Else	95
55. Of the Clothing and the Footgear of the Brethren	96
56. Of the Abbot's Table	98
57. Of the Artists of the Monastery	99
58. Of the Manner of Admitting Brethren	100
59. Of the Children of the Noble and of the Poor Who Are Offered	103
60. Of Priests Who May Wish to Live in the Monastery	105
61. How Stranger Monks Are to Be Received	107
62. Of the Priests of the Monastery	109
63. Of the Order in the Monastery	111
64. Of the Election of the Abbot	113
65. Of the Prior of the Monastery	115
66. Of the Porter of the Monastery	117
67. Of the Brethren Who Are Sent on a Journey	119
68. If a Brother Is Commanded to Do Impossible Things	120
69. That in the Monastery No One Presume to Defend Another	121
70. That No One Presume to Strike Another	122
71. That the Brethren Be Obedient to One Another	123
72. Of the Virtuous Zeal Which the Monks Ought to Have	124
73. Of This, that Not the Whole Observance of Righteousness Is Laid Down in this Rule	125

PROLOGUE

Listen, O my son, to the precepts of thy master, and incline the ear of thy heart, and cheerfully receive and faithfully execute the admonitions of thy loving Father, that by the toil of obedience thou mayest return to Him from whom by the sloth of disobedience thou hast gone away.

To thee, therefore, my speech is now directed, who, giving up thine own will, takest up the strong and most excellent arms of obedience, to do battle for Christ the Lord, the true King.

In the first place, beg of Him by most earnest prayer, that He perfect whatever good thou dost begin, in order that He who hath been pleased to count us in the number of His children, need never be grieved at our evil deeds. For we ought at all times so to serve Him with the good things which He hath given us, that He may not, like an angry father, disinherit his children, nor, like a dread lord, enraged at our evil deeds, hand us over to everlasting punishment as most wicked servants, who would not follow Him to glory.

Let us then rise at length, since the Scripture arouseth us, saying: "It is now the hour for us to rise from sleep" (Rom 13:11); and having opened our eyes to the deifying light, let us hear with awestruck ears what the divine voice, crying out daily, doth admonish us, saying: "Today, if you shall hear his voice, harden not your hearts" (Ps 94[95]:8). And again: "He that hath ears to hear let him hear what the Spirit saith to the churches" (Rev 2:7). And what doth He say?--"Come, children, hearken unto me, I will teach you the fear of the Lord" (Ps 33[34]:12). "Run whilst you have the light of life, that the darkness of death overtake you not" (Jn 12:35).

And the Lord seeking His workman in the multitude of the people, to whom He proclaimeth these words, saith again: "Who is the man that desireth life and loveth to see good days" (Ps 33[34]:13)? If hearing this thou answerest, "I am he," God saith to thee: "If thou wilt have true and everlasting life, keep thy tongue from evil, and thy lips from speaking guile; turn away from evil and do good; seek after peace and pursue it" (Ps 33[34]:14-15). And when you shall have done these things, my eyes shall be upon you, and my ears unto your prayers. And before you shall call upon me I will say: "Behold, I am here" (Is 58:9).

What, dearest brethren, can be sweeter to us than this voice of the Lord inviting us? See, in His loving kindness, the Lord showeth us the way of life. Therefore, having our loins girt with faith and the performance of good works, let us walk His ways under the guidance of the Gospel, that we may be found worthy of seeing Him who hath called us to His kingdom (cf 1 Thes 2:12).

If we desire to dwell in the tabernacle of His kingdom, we cannot reach it in any way, unless we run thither by good works.

But let us ask the Lord with the Prophet, saying to Him: "Lord, who shall dwell in Thy tabernacle, or who shall rest in Thy holy hill" (Ps 14[15]:1)?

After this question, brethren, let us listen to the Lord answering and showing us the way to this tabernacle, saying: "He that walketh without blemish and worketh justice; he that speaketh truth in his heart; who hath not used deceit in his tongue, nor hath done evil to his neighbor, nor hath taken up a reproach against his neighbor" (Ps 14[15]:2-3), who hath brought to naught the foul demon tempting him, casting him out of his heart with his temptation, and hath taken his evil thoughts whilst they were yet weak and hath dashed them against Christ (cf Ps 14[15]:4; Ps 136[137]:9); who fearing the Lord are not puffed up by their goodness of life, but holding that the actual good which is in them cannot be done by themselves, but by the Lord, they praise the Lord working in them (cf Ps 14[15]:4), saying with the Prophet: "Not to us, O Lord, not to us; by to Thy name give glory" (Ps 113[115:1]:9). Thus also the Apostle Paul hath not taken to himself any credit for his preaching, saying: "By the grace of God, I am what I am" (1 Cor 15:10). And again he saith: "He that glorieth, let him glory in the Lord" (2 Cor 10:17).

Hence, the Lord also saith in the Gospel: "He that heareth these my words and doeth them, shall be likened to a wise man who built his house upon a rock; the floods came, the winds blew, and they beat upon that house, and it fell not, for it was founded on a rock" (Mt 7:24-25). The Lord fulfilling these words waiteth for us from day to day, that we respond to His holy admonitions by our works. Therefore, our days are lengthened to a truce for the amendment of the misdeeds of our present life; as the Apostle saith: "Knowest thou not that the patience of God leadeth thee to penance" (Rom 2:4)? For the good Lord saith: "I will not the death of the sinner, but that he be converted and live" (Ezek 33:11).

Now, brethren, that we have asked the Lord who it is that shall dwell in His tabernacle, we have heard the conditions for dwelling there; and if we fulfil the duties of tenants, we shall be heirs of the kingdom of heaven. Our hearts and our bodies must, therefore, be ready to do battle under the biddings of holy obedience; and let us ask the Lord that He supply by the help of His grace what is impossible to us by nature. And if, flying from the pains of hell, we desire to reach life everlasting, then, while there is yet time, and we are still in the flesh, and are able during the present life to fulfil all these things, we must make haste to do now what will profit us forever.

We are, therefore, about to found a school of the Lord's service, in which we hope to introduce nothing harsh or burdensome. But even if, to correct vices or to preserve charity, sound reason dictateth anything that turneth out somewhat stringent, do not at once fly in dismay from the way of salvation, the beginning of which cannot but be narrow. But as we advance in the religious life and faith, we shall run the way of God's commandments with expanded hearts and unspeakable sweetness of love; so that never departing from His guidance and persevering in the monastery in His doctrine till death, we may by patience share in the sufferings of Christ, and be found worthy to be coheirs with Him of His kingdom.

1

OF THE KINDS OR THE LIFE OF MONKS

It is well known that there are four kinds of monks. The first kind is that of Cenobites, that is, the monastic, who live under a rule and an Abbot.

The second kind is that of Anchorites, or Hermits, that is, of those who, no longer in the first fervor of their conversion, but taught by long monastic practice and the help of many brethren, have already learned to fight against the devil; and going forth from the rank of their brethren well trained for single combat in the desert, they are able, with the help of God, to cope single-handed without the help of others, against the vices of the flesh and evil thoughts.

But a third and most vile class of monks is that of Sarabaites, who have been tried by no rule under the hand of a master, as gold is tried in the fire (cf Prov 27:21); but, soft as lead, and still keeping faith with the world by their works, they are known to belie God by their tonsure. Living in two's and three's, or even singly, without a shepherd, enclosed, not in the Lord's sheepfold, but in their own, the gratification of their desires is law unto them; because what they choose to do they call holy, but what they dislike they hold to be unlawful.

But the fourth class of monks is that called Landlopers, who keep going their whole life long from one province to another, staying three or four days at a time in different cells as guests. Always roving and never settled, they indulge their passions and the cravings of their appetite, and are in every way worse than the Sarabaites. It is better to pass all these over in silence than to speak of their most wretched life.

Therefore, passing these over, let us go on with the help of God to lay down a rule for that most valiant kind of monks, the Cenobites.

2

WHAT KIND OF MAN THE ABBOT OUGHT TO BE

The Abbot who is worthy to be over a monastery, ought always to be mindful of what he is called, and make his works square with his name of Superior. For he is believed to hold the place of Christ in the monastery, when he is called by his name, according to the saying of the Apostle: "You have received the spirit of adoption of sons, whereby we cry *Abba* (Father)" (Rom 8:15). Therefore, the Abbot should never teach, prescribe, or command (which God forbid) anything contrary to the laws of the Lord; but his commands and teaching should be instilled like a leaven of divine justice into the minds of his disciples.

Let the Abbot always bear in mind that he must give an account in the dread judgment of God of both his own teaching and of the obedience of his disciples. And let the Abbot know that whatever lack of profit the master of the house shall find in the sheep, will be laid to the blame of the shepherd. On the other hand he will be blameless, if he gave all a shepherd's care to his restless and unruly flock, and took all pains to correct their corrupt manners; so that their shepherd, acquitted at the Lord's judgment seat, may say to the Lord with the Prophet: "I have not hid Thy justice within my heart. I have declared Thy truth and Thy salvation" (Ps 39[40]:11). "But they contemning have despised me" (Is 1:2; Ezek 20:27). Then at length eternal death will be the crushing doom of the rebellious sheep under his charge.

When, therefore, anyone taketh the name of Abbot he should govern his disciples by a twofold teaching; namely, he should show them all that is good and holy by his deeds more than by his words; explain the commandments of God to intelligent disciples by words, but show the divine precepts to the dull and simple by his works. And let him show by his actions, that whatever he teacheth his disciples as being contrary to the law of God must not be done, "lest perhaps when he hath preached to others, he himself should become a castaway" (1 Cor 9:27), and he himself committing sin, God one day say to him: "Why dost thou declare My justices, and take My covenant in thy mouth? But thou hast hated discipline, and hast cast My words behind thee" (Ps 49[50]:16-17). And: "Thou who sawest the mote in thy brother's eye, hast not seen the beam in thine own" (Mt 7:3).

Let him make no distinction of persons in the monastery. Let him not love one more than another, unless it be one whom he findeth more exemplary in good works and obedience. Let not a free-born be preferred to a freedman, unless there be some other reasonable cause. But if from a just reason the Abbot deemeth it proper to make such a distinction, he may do so in regard to the rank of anyone whomsoever; otherwise let everyone keep his own place; for whether bond or free, we are all one in Christ (cf Gal 3:28; Eph 6:8), and we all bear an equal burden of servitude under one Lord, "for there is no respect of persons with God" (Rom 2:11). We are distinguished with Him in this respect alone, if we are found to excel others in good works and in humility. Therefore, let him have equal charity for all, and impose a uniform discipline for all according to merit.

For in his teaching the Abbot should always observe that principle of the Apostle in which he saith: "Reprove, entreat, rebuke" (2 Tm 4:2), that is, mingling gentleness with severity, as the occasion may call for, let him show the severity of the master and the loving affection of a father. He must sternly rebuke the undisciplined and restless; but he must exhort the obedient, meek, and patient to advance in virtue. But we charge him to rebuke and punish the negligent and haughty. Let him not shut his eyes to the sins of evil-doers; but on their first appearance let him do his utmost to cut them out from the root at once, mindful of the fate of Heli, the priest of Silo (cf 1 Samuel 2:11-4:18). The well-disposed and those of good understanding, let him correct at the first and second admonition only with words; but let him chastise the wicked and the hard of heart, and the proud and disobedient at the very first offense with stripes and other bodily punishments, knowing that it is written: "The fool is not corrected with words" (Prov 29:19). And again: "Strike thy son with the rod, and thou shalt deliver his soul from death" (Prov 23:14).

The Abbot ought always to remember what he is and what he is called, and to know that to whom much hath been entrusted, from him much will be required; and let him understand what a difficult and arduous task he assumeth in governing souls and accommodating himself to a variety of characters. Let him so adjust and adapt himself to everyone—to one gentleness of speech, to another by reproofs, and to still another by entreaties, to each one according to his bent and understanding—that he not only suffer no loss in his flock, but may rejoice in the increase of a worthy fold.

Above all things, that the Abbot may not neglect or undervalue the welfare of the souls entrusted to him, let him not have too great a concern about fleeting, earthly, perishable things; but let him always consider that he hath undertaken the government of souls, of which he must give an account. And that he may not perhaps complain of the want of earthly means, let him remember what is written: "Seek ye first the kingdom of God and His justice, and all these things shall be added unto you" (Mt 6:33). And again: "There is no want to them that fear Him" (Ps 33[34]:10). And let him know that he who undertaketh the government of souls must prepare himself to give an account for them; and whatever the number of brethren he hath under his charge, let him be sure that on judgment day he will, without doubt, have to give an account to the Lord for all these souls, in addition to that of his own. And thus, whilst he is in constant fear of the Shepherd's future examination about the sheep entrusted to him, and is watchful of his account for others, he is made solicitous also on his own account; and whilst by his admonitions he had administered correction to others, he is freed from his own failings.

3

OF CALLING THE BRETHREN FOR COUNSEL

Whenever weighty matters are to be transacted in the monastery, let the Abbot call together the whole community, and make known the matter which is to be considered. Having heard the brethren's views, let him weigh the matter with himself and do what he thinketh best. It is for this reason, however, we said that all should be called for counsel, because the Lord often revealeth to the younger what is best. Let the brethren, however, give their advice with humble submission, and let them not presume stubbornly to defend what seemeth right to them, for it must depend rather on the Abbot's will, so that all obey him in what he considereth best. But as it becometh disciples to obey their master, so also it becometh the master to dispose all things with prudence and justice. Therefore, let all follow the Rule as their guide in everything, and let no one rashly depart from it.

Let no one in the monastery follow the bent of his own heart, and let no one dare to dispute insolently with his Abbot, either inside or outside the monastery. If any one dare to do so, let him be placed under the correction of the Rule. Let the Abbot himself, however, do everything in the fear of the Lord and out of reverence for the Rule, knowing that, beyond a doubt, he will have to give an account to God, the most just Judge, for all his rulings. If, however, matters of less importance, having to do with the welfare of the monastery, are to be treated of, let him use the counsel of the Seniors only, as it is written: "Do all things with counsel, and thou shalt not repent when thou hast done" (Sir 32:24).

4

THE INSTRUMENTS OF GOOD WORKS

In the first place to love the Lord God with the whole heart, the whole soul, the whole strength..

(2) Then, one's neighbor as one's self (cf Mt 22:37-39; Mk 12:30-31; Lk 10:27).

(3) Then, not to kill...

(4) Not to commit adultery...

(5) Not to steal...

(6) Not to covet (cf Rom 13:9).

(7) Not to bear false witness (cf Mt 19:18; Mk 10:19; Lk 18:20).

(8) To honor all men (cf 1 Pt 2:17).

(9) And what one would not have done to himself, not to do to another (cf Tob 4:16; Mt 7:12; Lk 6:31).

(10) To deny one's self in order to follow Christ (cf Mt 16:24; Lk 9:23).

(11) To chastise the body (cf 1 Cor 9:27).

(12) Not to seek after pleasures.

(13) To love fasting.

(14) To relieve the poor.

(15) To clothe the naked...

(16) To visit the sick (cf Mt 25:36).

(17) To bury the dead.

(18) To help in trouble.

(19) To console the sorrowing.

(20) To hold one's self aloof from worldly ways.

(21) To prefer nothing to the love of Christ.

(22) Not to give way to anger.

(23) Not to foster a desire for revenge.

(24) Not to entertain deceit in the heart.

(25) Not to make a false peace.

(26) Not to forsake charity.

(27) Not to swear, lest perchance one swear falsely.

(28) To speak the truth with heart and tongue.

(29) Not to return evil for evil (cf 1 Thes 5:15; 1 Pt 3:9).

(30) To do no injury, yea, even patiently to bear the injury done us.

(31) To love one's enemies (cf Mt 5:44; Lk 6:27).

(32) Not to curse them that curse us, but rather to bless them.

(33) To bear persecution for justice sake (cf Mt 5:10).

(34) Not to be proud...

(35) Not to be given to wine (cf Ti 1:7; 1 Tm 3:3).

(36) Not to be a great eater.

(37) Not to be drowsy.

(38) Not to be slothful (cf Rom 12:11).

(39) Not to be a murmurer.

(40) Not to be a detractor.

(41) To put one's trust in God.

(42) To refer what good one sees in himself, not to self, but to God.

(43) But as to any evil in himself, let him be convinced that it is his own and charge it to himself.

(44) To fear the day of judgment.

(45) To be in dread of hell.

(46) To desire eternal life with all spiritual longing.

(47) To keep death before one's eyes daily.

(48) To keep a constant watch over the actions of our life.

(49) To hold as certain that God sees us everywhere.

(50) To dash at once against Christ the evil thoughts which rise in one's heart.

(51) And to disclose them to our spiritual father.

(52) To guard one's tongue against bad and wicked speech.

(53) Not to love much speaking.

(54) Not to speak useless words and such as provoke laughter.

(55) Not to love much or boisterous laughter.

(56) To listen willingly to holy reading.

(57) To apply one's self often to prayer.

(58) To confess one's past sins to God daily in prayer with sighs and tears, and to amend them for the future.

(59) Not to fulfil the desires of the flesh (cf Gal 5:16).

(60) To hate one's own will.

(61) To obey the commands of the Abbot in all things, even though he himself (which Heaven forbid) act otherwise, mindful of that precept of the Lord: "What they say, do ye; what they do, do ye not" (Mt 23:3).

(62) Not to desire to be called holy before one is; but to be holy first, that one may be truly so called.

(63) To fulfil daily the commandments of God by works.

(64) To love chastity.

(65) To hate no one.

(66) Not to be jealous; not to entertain envy.

(67) Not to love strife.

(68) Not to love pride.

(69) To honor the aged.

(70) To love the younger.

(71) To pray for one's enemies in the love of Christ.

(72) To make peace with an adversary before the setting of the sun.

(73) And never to despair of God's mercy.

Behold, these are the instruments of the spiritual art, which, if they have been applied without ceasing day and night and approved on judgment day, will merit for us from the Lord that reward which He hath promised: "The eye hath not seen, nor the ear heard, neither hath it entered into the heart of man, what things God hath prepared for them that love Him" (1 Cor 2:9). But the workshop in which we perform all these works with diligence is the enclosure of the monastery, and stability in the community.

5

OF OBEDIENCE

The first degree of humility is obedience without delay. This becometh those who, on account of the holy subjection which they have promised, or of the fear of hell, or the glory of life everlasting, hold nothing dearer than Christ. As soon as anything hath been commanded by the Superior they permit no delay in the execution, as if the matter had been commanded by God Himself. Of these the Lord saith: "At the hearing of the ear he hath obeyed Me" (Ps 17[18]:45). And again He saith to the teachers: "He that heareth you heareth Me" (Lk 10:16).

Such as these, therefore, instantly quitting their own work and giving up their own will, with hands disengaged, and leaving unfinished what they were doing, follow up, with the ready step of obedience, the work of command with deeds; and thus, as if in the same moment, both matters—the master's command and the disciple's finished work—are, in the swiftness of the fear of God, speedily finished together, whereunto the desire of advancing to eternal life urgeth them. They, therefore, seize upon the narrow way whereof the Lord saith: "Narrow is the way which leadeth to life" (Mt 7:14), so that, not living according to their own desires and pleasures but walking according to the judgment and will of another, they live in monasteries, and desire an Abbot to be over them. Such as these truly live up to the maxim of the Lord in which He saith: "I came not to do My own will, but the will of Him that sent Me" (Jn 6:38).

This obedience, however, will be acceptable to God and agreeable to men then only, if what is commanded is done without hesitation, delay, lukewarmness, grumbling or complaint, because the obedience which is rendered to Superiors is rendered to God. For He Himself hath said: "He that heareth you heareth Me" (Lk 10:16). And it must be rendered by the disciples with a good will, "for the Lord loveth a cheerful giver (2 Cor 9:7). " For if the disciple obeyeth with an ill will, and murmureth, not only with lips but also in his heart, even though he fulfils the command, yet it will not be acceptable to God, who regardeth the heart of the murmurer. And for such an action he acquireth no reward; rather he incurreth the penalty of murmurers, unless he maketh satisfactory amendment.

6

OF SILENCE

Let us do what the Prophet saith: "I said, I will take heed of my ways, that I sin not with my tongue: I have set a guard to my mouth, I was dumb, and was humbled, and kept silence even from good things" (Ps 38[39]:2-3). Here the prophet showeth that, if at times we ought to refrain from useful speech for the sake of silence, how much more ought we to abstain from evil words on account of the punishment due to sin.

Therefore, because of the importance of silence, let permission to speak be seldom given to perfect disciples even for good and holy and edifying discourse, for it is written: "In much talk thou shalt not escape sin" (Prov 10:19). And elsewhere: "Death and life are in the power of the tongue" (Prov 18:21). For it belongeth to the master to speak and to teach; it becometh the disciple to be silent and to listen. If, therefore, anything must be asked of the Superior, let it be asked with all humility and respectful submission. But coarse jests, and idle words or speech provoking laughter, we condemn everywhere to eternal exclusion; and for such speech we do not permit the disciple to open his lips.

7

OF HUMILITY

Brethren, the Holy Scripture crieth to us saying: "Every one that exalteth himself shall be humbled; and he that humbleth himself shall be exalted" (Lk 14:11; 18:14). Since, therefore, it saith this, it showeth us that every exaltation is a kind of pride. The Prophet declareth that he guardeth himself against this, saying: "Lord, my heart is not puffed up; nor are my eyes haughty. Neither have I walked in great matters nor in wonderful things above me" (Ps 130[131]:1). What then? "If I was not humbly minded, but exalted my soul; as a child that is weaned is towards his mother so shalt Thou reward my soul" (Ps 130[131]:2).

Hence, brethren, if we wish to reach the greatest height of humility, and speedily to arrive at that heavenly exaltation to which ascent is made in the present life by humility, then, mounting by our actions, we must erect the ladder which appeared to Jacob in his dream, by means of which angels were shown to him ascending and descending (cf Gen 28:12). Without a doubt, we understand this ascending and descending to be nothing else but that we descend by pride and ascend by humility. The erected ladder, however, is our life in the present world, which, if the heart is humble, is by the Lord lifted up to heaven. For we say that our body and our soul are the two sides of this ladder; and into these sides the divine calling hath inserted various degrees of humility or discipline which we must mount.

The first degree of humility, then, is that a man always have the fear of God before his eyes (cf Ps 35[36]:2), shunning all forgetfulness and that he be ever mindful of all that God hath commanded, that he always considereth in his mind how those who despise God will burn in hell for their sins, and that life everlasting is prepared for those who fear God. And whilst he guardeth himself evermore against sin and vices of thought, word, deed, and self-will, let him also hasten to cut off the desires of the flesh.

Let a man consider that God always seeth him from Heaven, that the eye of God beholdeth his works everywhere, and that the angels report them to Him every hour. The Prophet telleth us this when he showeth God thus ever present in our thoughts, saying: "The searcher of hearts and reins is God" (Ps 7:10). And again: "The Lord knoweth the thoughts of men" (Ps 93[94]:11) And he saith: "Thou hast understood my thoughts afar off" (Ps 138[139]:3). And: "The thoughts of man shall give praise to Thee" (Ps 75[76]:11). Therefore, in order that he may always be on his guard against evil thoughts, let the humble brother always say in his heart: "Then I shall be spotless before Him, if I shall keep myself from iniquity" (Ps 17[18]:24).

We are thus forbidden to do our own will, since the Scripture saith to us: "And turn away from thy evil will" (Sir 18:30). And thus, too, we ask God in prayer that His will may be done in us (cf Mt 6:10). We are, therefore, rightly taught not to do our own will, when we guard against what Scripture saith: "There are ways that to men seem right, the end whereof plungeth into the depths of hell" (Prov 16:25). And also when we are filled with dread at what is said of the negligent: "They are corrupted and become abominable in their pleasure" (Ps 13[14]:1). But as regards desires of the flesh, let us believe that God is thus ever present to us, since the Prophet saith to the Lord: "Before Thee is all my desire" (Ps 37[38]:10).

We must, therefore, guard thus against evil desires, because death hath his station near the entrance of pleasure. Whence the Scripture commandeth, saying: "Go no after thy lusts" (Sir 18:30). If, therefore, the eyes of the Lord observe the good and the bad (cf Prov 15:3) and the Lord always looketh down from heaven on the children of men, to see whether there be anyone that understandeth or seeketh God (cf Ps 13[14]:2); and if our actions are reported to the Lord day and night by the angels who are appointed to watch over us daily, we must ever be on our guard, brethren, as the Prophet saith in the psalm, that God may at no time see us "gone aside to evil and become unprofitable" (Ps 13[14]:3), and having spared us in the present time, because He is kind and waiteth for us to be changed for the better, say to us in the future: "These things thou hast done and I was silent" (Ps 49[50]:21).

The second degree of humility is, when a man loveth not his own will, nor is pleased to fulfill his own desires but by his deeds carrieth our that word of the Lord which saith: "I came not to do My own will but the will of Him that sent Me" (Jn 6:38). It is likewise said: "Self-will hath its punishment, but necessity winneth the crown."

The third degree of humility is, that for the love of God a

man subject himself to a Superior in all obedience, imitating the Lord, of whom the Apostle saith: "He became obedient unto death" (Phil 2:8).

The fourth degree of humility is, that, if hard and distasteful things are commanded, nay, even though injuries are inflicted, he accept them with patience and even temper, and not grow weary or give up, but hold out, as the Scripture saith: "He that shall persevere unto the end shall be saved" (Mt 10:22). And again: "Let thy heart take courage, and wait thou for the Lord" (Ps 26[27]:14). And showing that a faithful man ought even to bear every disagreeable thing for the Lord, it saith in the person of the suffering: "For Thy sake we suffer death all the day long; we are counted as sheep for the slaughter" (Rom 8:36; Ps 43[44]:22). And secure in the hope of the divine reward, they go on joyfully, saying: "But in all these things we overcome because of Him that hath loved us" (Rom 8:37). And likewise in another place the Scripture saith: "Thou, O God, hast proved us; Thou hast tried us by fire as silver is tried; Thou hast brought us into a net, Thou hast laid afflictions on our back" (Ps 65[66]:10-11). And to show us that we ought to be under a Superior, it continueth, saying: "Thou hast set men over our heads" (Ps 65[66]:12). And fulfilling the command of the Lord by patience also in adversities and injuries, when struck on the one cheek they turn also the other; the despoiler of their coat they give their cloak also; and when forced to go one mile they go two (cf Mt 5:39-41); with the Apostle Paul they bear with false brethren and "bless those who curse them" (2 Cor 11:26; 1 Cor 4:12).

The fifth degree of humility is, when one hideth from his Abbot none of the evil thoughts which rise in his heart or the evils committed by him in secret, but humbly confesseth them. Concerning this the Scripture exhorts us, saying: "Reveal thy way to the Lord and trust in Him" (Ps 36[37]:5). And it saith further: "Confess to the Lord, for He is good, for His mercy endureth forever" (Ps 105[106]:1; Ps 117[118]:1). And the Prophet likewise saith: "I have acknowledged my sin to Thee and my injustice I have not concealed. I said I will confess against myself my injustice to the Lord; and Thou hast forgiven the wickedness of my sins" (Ps 31[32]:5).

The sixth degree of humility is, when a monk is content with the meanest and worst of everything, and in all that is enjoined him holdeth himself as a bad and worthless workman, saying with the Prophet: "I am brought to nothing and I knew it not; I am become as a beast before Thee, and I am always with Thee" (Ps 72[73]:22-23).

The seventh degree of humility is, when, not only with his tongue he declareth, but also in his inmost soul believeth, that he is the lowest and vilest of men, humbling himself and saying with the Prophet: "But I am a worm and no man, the reproach of men and the outcast of the people" (Ps 21[22]:7). "I have been exalted and humbled and confounded" (Ps 87[88]:16). And also: "It is good for me that Thou hast humbled me, that I may learn Thy commandments" (Ps 118[119]:71,73).

The eighth degree of humility is, when a monk doeth nothing but what is sanctioned by the common rule of the monastery and the example of his elders.

The ninth degree of humility is, when a monk withholdeth his tongue from speaking, and keeping silence doth not speak until he is asked; for the Scripture showeth that "in a multitude of words there shall not want sin" (Prov 10:19); and that "a man full of tongue is not established in the earth" (Ps 139[140]:12).

The tenth degree of humility is, when a monk is not easily

moved and quick for laughter, for it is written: "The fool exalteth his voice in laughter" (Sir 21:23).

The eleventh degree of humility is, that, when a monk speaketh, he speak gently and without laughter, humbly and with gravity, with few and sensible words, and that he be not loud of voice, as it is written: "The wise man is known by the fewness of his words."

The twelfth degree of humility is, when a monk is not only humble of heart, but always letteth it appear also in his whole exterior to all that see him; namely, at the Work of God, in the garden, on a journey, in the field, or wherever he may be, sitting, walking, or standing, let him always have his head bowed down, his eyes fixed on the ground, ever holding himself guilty of his sins, thinking that he is already standing before the dread judgment seat of God, and always saying to himself in his heart what the publican in the Gospel said, with his eyes fixed on the ground: "Lord, I am a sinner and not worthy to lift up mine eyes to heaven" (Lk 18:13); and again with the Prophet: "I am bowed down and humbled exceedingly" (Ps 37[38]:7-9; Ps 118[119]:107).

Having, therefore, ascended all these degrees of humility, the monk will presently arrive at that love of God, which being perfect, casteth out fear (1 Jn 4:18). In virtue of this love all things which at first he observed not without fear, he will now begin to keep without any effort, and as it were, naturally by force of habit, no longer from the fear of hell, but from the love of Christ, from the very habit of good and the pleasure in virtue. May the Lord be pleased to manifest all this by His Holy Spirit in His laborer now cleansed from vice and sin.

8
OF THE DIVINE OFFICE DURING THE NIGHT

Making due allowance for circumstances, the brethren will rise during the winter season, that is, from the calends of November till Easter, at the eighth hour of the night; so that, having rested till a little after midnight, they may rise refreshed. The time, however, which remains over after the night office (Matins) will be employed in study by those of the brethren who still have some parts of the psalms and the lessons to learn.

But from Easter to the aforesaid calends, let the hour for celebrating the night office (Matins) be so arranged, that after a very short interval, during which the brethren may go out for the necessities of nature, the morning office (Lauds), which is to be said at the break of day, may follow presently.

9

HOW MANY PSALMS ARE TO BE SAID AT THE NIGHT OFFICE

During the winter season, having in the first place said the verse: *Deus, in adjutorium meum intende; Domine, ad adjuvandum me festina*, there is next to be said three times, *Domine, labia mea aperies, et os meum annuntiabit laudem tuam* (Ps 50[51]:17). To this the third psalm and the *Gloria* are to be added. After this the 94th psalm with its antiphon is to be said or chanted. Hereupon let a hymn follow, and after that six psalms with antiphons. When these and the verse have been said, let the Abbot give the blessing. All being seated on the benches, let three lessons be read alternately by the brethren from the book on the reading stand, between which let three responsories be said. Let two of the responsories be said without the *Gloria*, but after the third lesson, let him who is chanting say the *Gloria*. When the cantor beginneth to sing it, let all rise at once from their seats in honor and reverence of the Blessed Trinity.

Let the inspired books of both the Old and the New Testaments be read at the night offices, as also the expositions of them which have been made by the most eminent orthodox and Catholic Fathers.

After these three lessons with their responsories, let six other psalms follow, to be sung with *Alleluia*. After these let the lessons from the Apostle follow, to be said by heart, then the verse, the invocation of the litany, that is, *Kyrie eleison*. And thus let the night office come to an end.

10
HOW THE OFFICE IS TO BE SAID DURING THE SUMMER SEASON

From Easter till the calends of November let the whole psalmody, as explained above, be said, except that on account of the shortness of the nights, no lessons are read from the book; but instead of these three lessons, let one from the Old Testament be said from memory. Let a short responsory follow this, and let all the rest be performed as was said; namely, that never fewer than twelve psalms be said at the night office, exclusive of the third and the 94th psalm.

11

HOW THE NIGHT OFFICE IS TO BE SAID ON SUNDAYS

For the night office on Sunday the monks should rise earlier. At this office let the following regulations be observed, namely: after six psalms and the verse have been sung, as we arranged above, and all have been properly seated on the benches in their order, let four lessons with their responsories be read from the book, as we said above. In the fourth responsory only, let the *Gloria* be said by the chanter, and as soon as he beginneth it let all presently rise with reverence.

After these lessons let six other psalms with antiphons and the verse follow in order as before. After these let there be said three canticles from the Prophets, selected by the Abbot, and chanted with *Alleluia*. When the verse also hath been said and the Abbot hath given the blessing, let four other lessons from the New Testament be read in the order above mentioned. But after the fourth responsory let the Abbot intone the hymn *Te Deum laudamus*. When this hath been said, let the Abbot read the lesson from the Gospel, all standing with reverence and awe.

When the Gospel hath been read let all answer *Amen*, and immediately the Abbot will follow up with the hymn *Te decet laus*, and when he hath given the blessing Lauds will begin.

Let this order of the night office be observed on Sunday the same way in all seasons, in summer as well as in winter, unless perchance (which God forbid) the brethren should rise too late and part of the lessons or the responsories would have to be shortened. Let every precaution be taken that this does not occur. If it should happen, let him through whose neglect it came about make due satisfaction for it to God in the oratory.

12

HOW LAUDS ARE TO BE SAID

At Lauds on Sunday, let the 66th psalm be said first simply, without an antiphon. After that let the 50th psalm be said with *Alleluia*; after this let the 117th and the 62d be said; then the blessing and the praises, one lesson from the Apocalypse, said by heart, a responsory, the Ambrosian hymn, the verse and the canticle from the Gospel, the litany, and it is finished.

13

HOW LAUDS ARE TO BE SAID ON WEEK DAYS

On week days let Lauds be celebrated in the following manner, to wit: Let the 66th psalm be said without an antiphon, drawing it out a little as on Sunday, that all may arriver for the 50th, which is to be said with an antiphon. After this let two other psalms be said according to custom; namely, the 5th and the 35th on the second day, the 42d and the 56th on the third day, the 63rd and the 64th on the fourth day, the 87th and the 89th on the fifth day, the 75th and the 91st on the sixth day, and on Saturday the 142d and the canticle of Deuteronomy, which should be divided into two *Glorias*. On the other days, however, let the canticle from the Prophets, each for its proper day, be said as the Roman Church singeth it. After these let the psalms of praise follow; then one lesson from the Apostle, to be said from memory, the responsory, the Ambrosian hymn, the verse, the canticle from the Gospel, the litany, and it is finished.

Owing to the scandals which are wont to spring up, the

morning and the evening office should, plainly, never end unless the Lord's Prayer is said in the hearing of all by the Superior in its place at the end; so that in virtue of the promise which the brethren make when they say, "Forgive us as we forgive" (Mt 6:12), they may cleanse themselves of failings of this kind.

At the other hours which are to be said, however, let only the last part of this prayer be said aloud, so that all may answer, "But deliver us from evil" (Mt 6:13).

14
HOW THE NIGHT OFFICE IS TO BE SAID ON THE FEASTS OF THE SAINTS

On the feasts of the saints and on all solemn festivals let the night office be performed as we said it should be done on Sunday; except that the psalms, the antiphons, and the lessons proper for that day be said; but let the number above mentioned be maintained.

15

AT WHAT TIMES THE ALLELUIA IS TO BE SAID

From holy Easter until Pentecost let the *Alleluia* be said without intermission, both with the psalms and with the responsories; but from Pentecost until the beginning of Lent let it be said every night at the nocturns with the six latter psalms only. However, on all Sundays outside of Lent, let the canticles, Lauds, Prime, Tierce, Sext, and None be said with *Alleluia*. Let Vespers, however, be said with the antiphon; but let the responsories never be said with *Alleluia*, except from Easter to Pentecost.

16

HOW THE WORK OF GOD IS TO BE PERFORMED DURING THE DAY

As the Prophet saith: "Seven times a day I have given praise to Thee" (Ps 118[119]:164), this sacred sevenfold number will be fulfilled by us in this wise if we perform the duties of our service at the time of Lauds, Prime, Tierce, Sext, None, Vespers, and Complin; because it was of these day hours that he hath said: "Seven times a day I have given praise to Thee" (Ps 118[119]:164). For the same Prophet saith of the night watches: "At midnight I arose to confess to Thee" (Ps 118[119]:62). At these times, therefore, let us offer praise to our Creator "for the judgments of His justice;" namely, at Lauds, Prime, Tierce, Sext, None, Vespers, and Complin; and let us rise at night to praise Him (cf Ps 118[119]:164, 62).

17

HOW MANY PSALMS ARE TO BE SUNG AT THESE HOURS

We have now arranged the order of the psalmody for the night and the morning office; let us next arrange for the succeeding Hours. At the first Hour let three psalms be said separately, and not under one *Gloria*. Let the hymn for the same Hour be said after the verse *Deus, in adjutorium* (Ps 69[70]:2), before the psalms are begun. Then, after the completion of three psalms, let one lesson be said, a verse, the *Kyrie eleison*, and the collects.

At the third, the sixth, and the ninth Hours, the prayer will be said in the same order; namely, the verse, the hymn proper to each Hour, the three psalms, the lesson, the verse, the *Kyrie eleison*, and the collects. If the brotherhood is large, let these Hours be sung with antiphons; but if small, let them be said without a break.

Let the office of Vespers be ended with four psalms and antiphons; after these psalms a lesson is to be recited, next a responsory, the Ambrosian hymn, a verse, the canticle from the Gospel, the litany, the Lord's Prayer, and the collects.

Let Complin end with the saying of three psalms, which are to be said straight on without an antiphon, and after these the hymn for the same Hour, one lesson, the verse, *Kyrie eleison*, the blessing, and the collects.

18

IN WHAT ORDER THE PSALMS ARE TO BE SAID

In the beginning let there be said the verse, *Deus, in adjutorium meum intende; Domine, ad adjuvandum me festina* (Ps 69[70]:2), and the *Gloria*, followed by the hymn for each Hour. At Prime on Sunday, then, there are to be said four sections of the 118th psalm. At the other Hours, however, namely Tierce, Sext, and None, let three sections of the same psalm be said. But at Prime on Monday let three psalms be said, namely, the first, the second, and the sixth; and thus each day at Prime until Sunday, let three psalms be said each time in consecutive order up to the 19th psalm, yet so that the ninth psalm and the 17th be each divided into two *Glorias*; and thus it will come about that at the night office on Sundays we always begin with the 20th psalm.

At Tierce, Sext, and None, on Monday, however, let the nine sections which remain over the 118th psalm be said, three sections at each of these Hours. The 118th psalm having thus been parceled out for two days, namely, Sunday and Monday, let there be sung on Tuesday for Tierce, Sext, and None, three psalms each, from the 119th to the 127th, that is, nine psalms. These psalms will always be repeated at the same Hours in just the same way until Sunday, observing also for all these days a regular succession of the hymns, the lessons, and the verses, so, namely, that on Sunday the beginning is always made with the 118th psalm.

Let Vespers be sung daily with the singing of four psalms. Let these psalms begin with the 109th to the 147th, excepting those which are set aside for the other Hours; namely, from the 117th to the 127th, and the 133d, and the 142d. All the rest are to be said at Vespers; and as the psalms fall three short, those of the aforesaide psalms which are found to be longer, are to be divided; namely, the 138th, the 143d, and the 144th. But because the 116th is short, let it be joined to the 115th. The order of the psalms for Vespers having thus been arranged let the rest, namely, the lessons, the responsories, the hymns, the verses, and the canticles, be said as we have directed above.

At Complin, however, let the same psalms be repeated every day; namely, the 4th, the 90th, and the 133d.

Having arranged the order of the office, let all the rest of the psalms which remain over, be divided equally into seven night offices, by so dividing such of them as are of greater length that twelve fall to each night. We especially impress this, that, if this distribution of the psalms should perchance displease anyone, he arrange them if he thinketh another better, by all means seeing to it that the whole Psalter of one hundred and fifty psalms be said every week, and that it always start again from the beginning at Matins on Sunday; because those monks show too lax a service in their devotion who in the course of a week chant less than the whole Psalter with is customary canticles; since we read, that our holy forefathers promptly fulfilled in one day what we lukewarm monks should, please God, perform at least in a week.

19

OF THE MANNER OF RECITING THE PSALTER

We believe that God is present everywhere and that the eyes of the Lord behold the good and the bad in every place (cf Prov 15:3). Let us firmly believe this, especially when we take part in the Work of God. Let us, therefore, always be mindful of what the Prophet saith, "Serve ye the Lord with fear" (Ps 2:11). And again, "Sing ye wisely" (Ps 46[47]:8). And, "I will sing praise to Thee in the sight of the angels" (Ps 137[138]:1). Therefore, let us consider how it becometh us to behave in the sight of God and His angels, and let us so stand to sing, that our mind may be in harmony with our voice.

20

OF REVERENCE AT PRAYER

If we do not venture to approach men who are in power, except with humility and reverence, when we wish to ask a favor, how much must we beseech the Lord God of all things with all humility and purity of devotion? And let us be assured that it is not in many words, but in the purity of heart and tears of compunction that we are heard. For this reason prayer ought to be short and pure, unless, perhaps it is lengthened by the inspiration of divine grace. At the community exercises, however, let the prayer always be short, and the sign having been given by the Superior, let all rise together.

21

OF THE DEANS OF THE MONASTERY

If the brotherhood is large, let brethren of good repute and holy life be chosen from among them and be appointed Deans; and let them take care of their deaneries in everything according to the commandments of God and the directions of their Abbot. Let such be chosen Deans as the Abbot may safely trust to share his burden. Let them not be chosen for their rank, but for the merit of their life and their wisdom and knowledge; and if any of them, puffed up with pride, should be found blameworthy and, after having been corrected once and again and even a third time, refuseth to amend, let him be deposed, and one who is worthy be placed in his stead. We make the same regulation with reference to the Prior.

22

HOW THE MONKS ARE TO SLEEP

Let the brethren sleep singly, each in a separate bed. Let them receive the bedding befitting their mode of life, according to the direction of their Abbot. If it can be done, let all sleep in one apartment; but if the number doth not allow it, let them sleep in tens or twenties with the seniors who have charge of them. Let a light be kept burning constantly in the cell till morning.

Let them sleep clothed and girded with cinctures or cords, that they may be always ready; but let them not have knives at their sides whilst they sleep, lest perchance the sleeping be wounded in their dreams; and the sign having been given, rising without delay, let them hasten to outstrip each other to the Work of God, yet with all gravity and decorum. Let the younger brethren not have their beds beside each other, but intermingled with the older ones; and rising to the Work of God, let them gently encourage one another on account of the excuses of the drowsy.

23

OF EXCOMMUNICATION FOR FAULTS

If a brother is found stubborn or disobedient or proud or murmuring, or opposed to anything in the Holy Rule and a contemner of the commandments of his Superiors, let him be admonished by his Superiors once and again in secret, according to the command of our Lord (cf Mt 18:15-16). If he doth not amend let him be taken to task publicly before all. But if he doth not reform even then, and he understandeth what a penalty it is, let him be placed under excommunication; but if even then he remaineth obstinate let him undergo corporal punishment.

24

WHAT THE MANNER OF EXCOMMUNICATION SHOULD BE

The degree of excommunication or punishment ought to be meted out according to the gravity of the offense, and to determine that is left to the judgment of the Abbot. If, however, anyone of the brethren is detected in smaller faults, let him be debarred from eating at the common table.

The following shall be the practice respecting one who is excluded from the common table: that he does not intone a psalm or an antiphon nor read a lesson in the oratory until he hath made satisfaction; let him take his meal alone, after the refection of the brethren; thus: if, for instance, the brethren take their meal at the sixth hour that brother will take his at the ninth, and if the brethren take theirs at the ninth, he will take his in the evening, until by due satisfaction he obtaineth pardon.

25

OF GRAVER FAULTS

But let the brother who is found guilty of a graver fault be excluded from both the table and the oratory. Let none of the brethren join his company or speak with him. Let him be alone at the work enjoined on him, persevering in penitential sorrow, mindful of the terrible sentence of the Apostle who saith, that "such a man is delivered over for the destruction of the flesh, that the spirit may be saved in the day of the Lord" (1 Cor 5:5). Let him get his food alone in such quantity and at such a time as the Abbot shall deem fit; and let him not be blessed by anyone passing by, nor the food that is given him.

26
OF THOSE WHO WITHOUT THE COMMAND OF THE ABBOT ASSOCIATE WITH THE EXCOMMUNICATED

If any brother presume to associate with an excommunicated brother in any way, or to speak with him, or to send him a message, without the command of the Abbot, let him incur the same penalty of excommunication.

27

HOW CONCERNED THE ABBOT SHOULD BE ABOUT THE EXCOMMUNICATED

Let the Abbot show all care and concern towards offending brethren because "they that are in health need not a physician, but they that are sick" (Mt 9:12). Therefore, like a prudent physician he ought to use every opportunity to send consolers, namely, discreet elderly brethren, to console the wavering brother, as it were, in secret, and induce him to make humble satisfaction; and let them cheer him up "lest he be swallowed up with overmuch sorrow" (2 Cor 2:7); but, as the same Apostle saith, "confirm your charity towards him" (2 Cor 2:8); and let prayer be said for him by all.

The Abbot must take the utmost pains, and strive with all prudence and zeal, that none of the flock entrusted to him perish. For the Abbot must know that he has taken upon himself the care of infirm souls, not a despotism over the strong; and let him fear the threat of the Prophet wherein the Lord saith: "What ye saw to be fat, that ye took to yourselves, and what was diseased you threw away" (Ezek 34:3-4). And let him follow the loving example of the Good Shepherd, who, leaving the ninety-nine sheep on the mountains, went to seek the one that had gone astray, on whose weakness He had such pity, that He was pleased to lay it on His sacred shoulders and thus carry it back to the fold (cf Lk 15:5).

28

OF THOSE WHO HAVING OFTEN BEEN CORRECTED DO NOT AMEND

If a brother hath often been corrected and hath even been excommunicated for a fault and doth not amend, let a more severe correction be applied to him, namely, proceed against him with corporal punishment.

But if even then he doth not reform, or puffed up with pride, should perhaps, which God forbid, even defend his actions, then let the Abbot act like a prudent physician. After he hath applied soothing lotions, ointments of admonitions, medicaments of the Holy Scriptures, and if, as a last resource, he hath employed the caustic of excommunication and the blows of the lash, and seeth that even then his pains are of no avail, let him apply for that brother also what is more potent than all these measures: his own prayer and that of the brethren, that the Lord who is all-powerful may work a cure in that brother.

But if he is not healed even in this way, then finally let the Abbot dismiss him from the community, as the Apostle saith:

"Put away the evil one from among you" (1 Cor 5:13); and again: "If the faithless depart, let him depart" (1 Cor 7:15); lest one diseased sheep infect the whole flock.

29

WHETHER BRETHREN WHO LEAVE THE MONASTERY OUGHT TO BE RECEIVED AGAIN

If a brother, who through his own fault leaveth the monastery or is expelled, desireth to return, let him first promise full amendment of the fault for which he left; and thus let him be received in the last place, that by this means his humility may be tried. If he should leave again, let him be received even a third time, knowing that after this every means of return will be denied him.

30
HOW YOUNG BOYS ARE TO BE CORRECTED

Every age and understanding should have its proper discipline. Whenever, therefore, boys or immature youths or such as can not understand how grave a penalty excommunication is, are guilty of a serious fault, let them undergo severe fasting or be disciplined with corporal punishment, that they may be corrected.

31

THE KIND OF MAN THE CELLARER OF THE MONASTERY OUGHT TO BE

Let there be chosen from the brotherhood as Cellarer of the monastery a wise man, of settled habits, temperate and frugal, not conceited, irritable, resentful, sluggish, or wasteful, but fearing God, who may be as a father to the whole brotherhood.

Let him have the charge of everything, let him do nothing without the command of the Abbot, let him do what hath been ordered him and not grieve the brethren. If a brother should perchance request anything of him unreasonably let him not sadden the brother with a cold refusal, but politely and with humility refuse him who asketh amiss. Let him be watchful of his own soul, always mindful of the saying of the Apostle: "For they that have ministered well, shall purchase to themselves a good degree" (1 Tm 3:13). Let him provide for the sick, the children, the guests, and the poor, with all care, knowing that, without doubt, he will have to give an account of all these things on judgment day. Let him regard all the vessels of the monastery and all its substance, as if they were sacred vessels of the altar. Let him neglect nothing and let him not give way to avarice, nor let him be wasteful and a squanderer of the goods of the monastery; but let him do all things in due measure and according to the bidding of his Abbot.

Above all things, let him be humble; and if he hath not the things to give, let him answer with a kind word, because it is written: "A good word is above the best gift" (Sir 18:17). Let him have under his charge everything that the Abbot hath entrusted to him, and not presume to meddle with matters forbidden him. Let him give the brethren their apportioned allowance without a ruffle or delay, that they may not be scandalized, mindful of what the Divine Word declareth that he deserveth who shall scandalize one of these little ones: "It were better for him that a millstone were hanged about his neck and that he were drowned in the depth of the sea" (Mt 18:6).

If the community is large, let assistants be given him, that, with their help, he too may fulfil the office entrusted to him with an even temper. Let the things that are to be given be distributed, and the things that are to be gotten asked for at the proper times, so that nobody may be disturbed or grieved in the house of God.

32

OF THE TOOLS AND GOODS OF THE MONASTERY

Let the Abbot appoint brethren on whose life and character he can rely, over the property of the monastery in tools, clothing, and things generally, and let him assign to them, as he shall deem proper, all the articles which must be collected after use and stored away. Let the Abbot keep a list of these articles, so that, when the brethren in turn succeed each other in these trusts, he may know what he giveth and what he receiveth back. If anyone, however, handleth the goods of the monastery slovenly or carelessly let him be reprimanded and if he doth not amend let him come under the discipline of the Rule.

33

WHETHER MONKS OUGHT TO HAVE ANYTHING OF THEIR OWN

The vice of personal ownership must by all means be cut out in the monastery by the very root, so that no one may presume to give or receive anything without the command of the Abbot; nor to have anything whatever as his own, neither a book, nor a writing tablet, nor a pen, nor anything else whatsoever, since monks are allowed to have neither their bodies nor their wills in their own power. Everything that is necessary, however, they must look for from the Father of the monastery; and let it not be allowed for anyone to have anything which the Abbot did not give or permit him to have. Let all things be common to all, as it is written. And let no one call or take to himself anything as his own (cf Acts 4:32). But if anyone should be found to indulge this most baneful vice, and, having been admonished once and again, doth not amend, let him be subjected to punishment.

34

WHETHER ALL SHOULD RECEIVE IN EQUAL MEASURE WHAT IS NECESSARY

It is written, "Distribution was made to everyone according as he had need" (Acts 4:35). We do not say by this that respect should be had for persons (God forbid), but regard for infirmities. Let him who hath need of less thank God and not give way to sadness, but let him who hath need of more, humble himself for his infirmity, and not be elated for the indulgence shown him; and thus all the members will be at peace.

Above all, let not the evil of murmuring appear in the least word or sign for any reason whatever. If anyone be found guilty herein, let him be placed under very severe discipline.

35

OF THE WEEKLY SERVERS IN THE KITCHEN

Let the brethren serve each other so that no one be excused from the work in the kitchen, except on account of sickness or more necessary work, because greater merit and more charity is thereby acquired. Let help be given to the weak, however, that they may not do this work with sadness; but let all have help according to the size of the community and the circumstances of the place. If the community is large, let the Cellarer be excused from the kitchen, or if, as we have said, any are engaged in more urgent work; let the rest serve each other in charity.

Let him who is to go out of the weekly service, do the cleaning on Saturday. Let him wash the towels with which the brethren wipe their hands and feet. Let him who goeth out, as well as him who is to come in, wash the feet of all. Let him return the utensils of his department to the Cellarer clean and whole. Let the Cellarer give the same to the one who cometh in, so that he may know what he giveth and what he receiveth back.

An hour before meal time let the weekly servers receive each a cup of drink and a piece of bread over the prescribed portion, that they may serve their brethren at the time time of refection without murmuring and undue strain. On solemn feast days, however, let them abstain till after Mass.

As soon as the morning office on Sunday is ended, let the weekly servers who come in and who go out, cast themselves upon their knees in the oratory before all, asking their prayers. Let him who goeth out of the weekly service, say the following verse: *Benedictus es, Domine Deus, qui adjuvisti me et consolatus se me* (Dan 3:52; Ps 85[86]:17). The one going out having said this three times and received the blessing, let the one who cometh in follow and say: *Deus in adjutorium meum intende; Domine, ad adjuvandum me festina* (Ps 69[70]:2). And let this also be repeated three times by all, and having received the blessing let him enter upon his weekly service.

36
OF THE SICK BRETHREN

Before and above all things, care must be taken of the sick, that they be served in very truth as Christ is served; because He hath said, "I was sick and you visited Me" (Mt 25:36). And "As long as you did it to one of these My least brethren, you did it to Me" (Mt 25:40). But let the sick themselves also consider that they are served for the honor of God, and let them not grieve their brethren who serve them by unnecessary demands. These must, however, be patiently borne with, because from such as these a more bountiful reward is gained. Let the Abbot's greatest concern, therefore, be that they suffer no neglect.

Let a cell be set apart for the sick brethren, and a God-fearing, diligent, and careful attendant be appointed to serve them. Let the use of the bath be offered to the sick as often as it is useful, but let it be granted more rarely to the healthy and especially the young. Thus also let the use of meat be granted to the sick and to the very weak for their recovery. But when they have been restored let them all abstain from meat in the usual manner.

But let the Abbot exercise the utmost care that the sick are not neglected by the Cellarer or the attendants, because whatever his disciples do amiss falleth back on him.

37

OF THE AGED AND CHILDREN

Although human nature is of itself drawn to feel compassion for these life-periods, namely, old age and childhood, still, let the decree of the Rule make provision also for them. Let their natural weakness be always taken into account and let the strictness of the Rule not be kept with them in respect to food, but let there be a tender regard in their behalf and let them eat before regular hours.

38

OF THE WEEKLY READER

Reading must not be wanting at the table of the brethren when they are eating. Neither let anyone who may chance to take up the book venture to read there; but let him who is to read for the whole week enter upon that office on Sunday. After Mass and Communion let him ask all to pray for him that God may ward off from him the spirit of pride. And let the following verse be said three times by all in the oratory, he beginning it: *Domine, labia mea aperies, et os meum annuntiabit laudem tuam* (Ps 50[51]:17), and thus having received the blessing let him enter upon the reading.

Let the deepest silence be maintained that no whispering or voice be heard except that of the reader alone. But let the brethren so help each other to what is needed for eating and drinking, that no one need ask for anything. If, however, anything should be wanted, let it be asked for by means of a sign of any kind rather than a sound. And let no one presume to ask any questions there, either about the book or anything else, in order that no cause to speak be given [to the devil] (Eph 4:27; 1 Tm 5:14), unless, perchance, the Superior wisheth to say a few words for edification.

Let the brother who is reader for the week take a little bread and wine before he beginneth to read, on account of Holy Communion, and lest it should be too hard for him to fast so long. Afterward, however, let him take his meal in the kitchen with the weekly servers and the waiters. The brethren, however, will not read or sing in order, but only those who edify their hearers.

39

OF THE QUANTITY OF FOOD

Making allowance for the infirmities of different persons, we believe that for the daily meal, both at the sixth and the ninth hour, two kinds of cooked food are sufficient at all meals; so that he who perchance cannot eat of one, may make his meal of the other. Let two kinds of cooked food, therefore, be sufficient for all the brethren. And if there be fruit or fresh vegetables, a third may be added. Let a pound of bread be sufficient for the day, whether there be only one meal or both dinner and supper. If they are to eat supper, let a third part of the pound be reserved by the Cellarer and be given at supper.

If, however, the work hath been especially hard, it is left to the discretion and power of the Abbot to add something, if he think fit, barring above all things every excess, that a monk be not overtaken by indigestion. For nothing is so contrary to Christians as excess, as our Lord saith: "See that your hearts be not overcharged with surfeiting" (Lk 21:34).

Let the same quantity of food, however, not be served out to young children but less than to older ones, observing measure in all things.

But let all except the very weak and the sick abstain altogether from eating the flesh of four-footed animals.

40

OF THE QUANTITY OF DRINK

"Every one hath his proper gift from God, one after this manner and another after that" (1 Cor 7:7). It is with some hesitation, therefore, that we determine the measure of nourishment for others. However, making allowance for the weakness of the infirm, we think one hemina of wine a day is sufficient for each one. But to whom God granteth the endurance of abstinence, let them know that they will have their special reward. If the circumstances of the place, or the work, or the summer's heat should require more, let that depend on the judgment of the Superior, who must above all things see to it, that excess or drunkenness do not creep in.

Although we read that wine is not at all proper for monks, yet, because monks in our times cannot be persuaded of this, let us agree to this, at least, that we do not drink to satiety, but sparingly; because "wine maketh even wise men fall off" (Sir 19:2). But where the poverty of the place will not permit the aforesaid measure to be had, but much less, or none at all, let those who live there bless God and murmur not. This we charge above all things, that they live without murmuring.

41

AT WHAT TIMES THE BRETHREN SHOULD TAKE THEIR REFECTION

From holy Easter till Pentecost let the brethren dine at the sixth hour and take supper in the evening. From Pentecost on, however, during the whole summer, if the monks have no work in the fields and the excess of the heat doth not interfere, let them fast on Wednesday and Friday until the ninth hour; but on the other days let them dine at the sixth hour. This sixth hour for dinner is to be continued, if they have work in the fields or the heat of the summer is great. Let the Abbot provide for this; and so let him manage and adapt everything that souls may be saved, and that what the brethren do, they may do without having a reasonable cause to murmur. From the ides of September until the beginning of Lent let them always dine at the ninth hour. During Lent, however, until Easter, let them dine in the evening. But let this evening hour be so arranged that they will not need lamp-light during their meal; but let everything be finished whilst it is still day. But at all times let the hour of meals, whether for dinner or for supper, be so arranged that everything is done by daylight.

42

THAT NO ONE SPEAK AFTER COMPLIN

Monks should always be given to silence, especially, however, during the hours of the night. Therefore, on every day, whether of fast or of a mid-day meal, as soon as they have risen from their evening meal, let all sit together in one place, and let one read the Conferences or the Lives of the Fathers, or something else that will edify the hearers; not, however, the Heptateuch or the Books of the Kings, because it would not be wholesome for weak minds to hear this part of the Scripture at that hour; they should, however, be read at other times. But if it was a fast-day, then, when Vespers have been said, and after a short interval, let them next come together for the reading of the Conferences, as we have said; and when the four or five pages have been read, or as much as the hour will permit, and all have assembled in one place during the time of the reading, let him also come who was perchance engaged in work enjoined on him. All, therefore, having assembled in one place, let them say Complin, and after going out from Complin, let there be no more permission from that time on for anyone to say anything.

If, however, anyone is found to break this rule, let him undergo heavy punishment, unless the needs of guests should arise, or the Abbot should perhaps give a command to anyone. But let even this be done with the utmost gravity and moderation.

43

OF THOSE WHO ARE TARDY IN COMING TO THE WORK OF GOD OR TO TABLE

As soon as the signal for the time of the divine office is heard, let everyone, leaving whatever he hath in his hands, hasten with all speed, yet with gravity, that there may be no cause for levity. Therefore, let nothing be preferred to the Work of God. If at Matins anyone cometh after the *Gloria* of the 94th psalm, which on that account we wish to be much drawn out and said slowly, let him not stand in his place in the choir; but let him stand last of all, or in a place which the Abbot hath set apart for such careless ones, that he may be seen by him and by all, until, the Work of God being ended, he maketh satisfaction by public penance. The reason, however, why we think they should stand in the last place, or apart from the rest, is this, that seen by all they may amend for very shame. For if they stayed outside the oratory, there might be one who would go back to sleep, or anyhow would seat himself outside, indulge in vain gossip, and give a "chance to the devil" (Eph

4:27; 1 Tm 5:14). Let him go inside, therefore, that he may not lose the whole, and may amend for the future.

At the day hours, however, whoever doth not arrive for the Work of God after the verse and the *Gloria* of the first psalm, which is said after the verse, let him stand in the last place, according to the rule which we stated above; and let him not attempt to join the choir of the chanters until he hath made satisfaction, unless, perchance, the Abbot's permission hath given him leave to do so, with the understanding that he atone the fault afterwards.

If anyone doth not come to table before the verse, so that all may say the verse and pray together and sit down to table at the same time, let him be twice corrected for this, if he failed to come through his own fault and negligence. If he doth not amend after this, let him not be permitted to eat at the common table; but separated from the company of all, let him eat alone, his portion of wine being taken from him, until he hath made satisfaction and hath amended. In like manner let him suffer who is not present also at the verse which is said after the refection.

And let no one presume to take food or drink before or after the appointed time. But if anything should be offered to a brother by the Superior and he refuseth to accept it, and afterwards desireth what at first he refused or anything else, let him receive nothing at all, until he maketh due satisfaction.

44

OF THOSE WHO ARE EXCOMMUNICATED—HOW THEY MAKE SATISFACTION

Whoever is excommunicated for graver faults from the oratory and the table, let him, at the time that the Work of God is celebrated in the oratory, lie stretched, face down in silence before the door of the oratory at the feet of all who pass out. And let him do this until the Abbot judgeth that it is enough. When he then cometh at the Abbot's bidding, let him cast himself at the Abbot's feet, then at the feet of all, that they may pray for him. If then the Abbot ordereth it, let him be received back into the choir in the place which the Abbot shall direct; yet so that he doth not presume to intone a psalm or a lesson or anything else in the oratory, unless the Abbot again biddeth him to do so. Then, at all the Hours, when the Work of God is ended, let him cast himself on the ground in the place where he standeth, and thus let him make satisfaction, until the Abbot again biddeth him finally to cease from this penance.

But let those who are excommunicated for lighter faults from the table only make satisfaction in the oratory, as long as the Abbot commandeth, and let them perform this until he giveth his blessing and saith, "It is enough."

45

OF THOSE WHO COMMIT A FAULT IN THE ORATORY

If anyone whilst he reciteth a psalm, a responsory, an antiphon, or a lesson, maketh a mistake, and doth not humble himself there before all by making satisfaction, let him undergo a greater punishment, because he would not correct by humility what he did amiss through negligence. But let children be beaten for such a fault.

46

OF THOSE WHO FAIL IN ANY OTHER MATTERS

If anyone whilst engaged in any work, in the kitchen, in the cellar, in serving, in the bakery, in the garden, at any art or work in any place whatever, committeth a fault, or breaketh or loseth anything, or transgresseth in any way whatever, and he doth not forthwith come before the Abbot and the community, and of his own accord confess his offense and make satisfaction, and it becometh known through another, let him be subjected to a greater correction.

If, however, the cause of the offense is secret, let him disclose it to the Abbot alone, or to his spiritual Superiors, who know how to heal their own wounds, and not expose and make public those of others.

47
OF GIVING THE SIGNAL FOR THE TIME OF THE WORK OF GOD

Let it be the Abbot's care that the time for the Work of God be announced both by day and by night; either to announce it himself, or to entrust this charge to a careful brother that everything may be done at the proper time.

Let those who have been ordered, intone the psalms or the antiphons in their turn after the Abbot. No one, however, should presume to sing or read unless he is able so to perform this office that the hearers may be edified; and let it be done with humility, gravity, and reverence by him whom the Abbot hath ordered.

48

OF THE DAILY WORK

Idleness is the enemy of the soul; and therefore the brethren ought to be employed in manual labor at certain times, at others, in devout reading. Hence, we believe that the time for each will be properly ordered by the following arrangement; namely, that from Easter till the calends of October, they go out in the morning from the first till about the fourth hour, to do the necessary work, but that from the fourth till about the sixth hour they devote to reading. After the sixth hour, however, when they have risen from table, let them rest in their beds in complete silence; or if, perhaps, anyone desireth to read for himself, let him so read that he doth not disturb others. Let None be said somewhat earlier, about the middle of the eighth hour; and then let them work again at what is necessary until Vespers.

If, however, the needs of the place, or poverty should require that they do the work of gathering the harvest themselves, let them not be downcast, for then are they monks in truth, if they live by the work of their hands, as did also our forefathers and the Apostles. However, on account of the faint-hearted let all things be done with moderation.

From the calends of October till the beginning of Lent, let them apply themselves to reading until the second hour complete. At the second hour let Tierce be said, and then let all be employed in the work which hath been assigned to them till the ninth hour. When, however, the first signal for the hour of None hath been given, let each one leave off from work and be ready when the second signal shall strike. But after their repast let them devote themselves to reading or the psalms.

During the Lenten season let them be employed in reading from morning until the third hour, and till the tenth hour let them do the work which is imposed on them. During these days of Lent let all receive books from the library, and let them read them through in order. These books are to be given out at the beginning of the Lenten season.

Above all, let one or two of the seniors be appointed to go about the monastery during the time that the brethren devote to reading and take notice, lest perhaps a slothful brother be found who giveth himself up to idleness or vain talk, and doth not attend to his reading, and is unprofitable, not only to himself, but disturbeth also others. If such a one be found (which God forbid), let him be punished once and again. If he doth not amend, let him come under the correction of the Rule in such a way that others may fear. And let not brother join brother at undue times.

On Sunday also let all devote themselves to reading, except those who are appointed to the various functions. But if anyone should be so careless and slothful that he will not or cannot meditate or read, let some work be given him to do, that he may not be idle.

Let such work or charge be given to the weak and the sickly brethren, that they are neither idle, nor so wearied with the strain of work that they are driven away. Their weakness must be taken into account by the Abbot.

49

ON THE KEEPING OF LENT

The life of a monk ought always to be a Lenten observance. However, since such virtue is that of few, we advise that during these days of Lent he guard his life with all purity and at the same time wash away during these holy days all the shortcomings of other times. This will then be worthily done, if we restrain ourselves from all vices. Let us devote ourselves to tearful prayers, to reading and compunction of heart, and to abstinence.

During these days, therefore, let us add something to the usual amount of our service, special prayers, abstinence from food and drink, that each one offer to God "with the joy of the Holy Ghost" (1 Thes 1:6), of his own accord, something above his prescribed measure; namely, let him withdraw from his body somewhat of food, drink, sleep, speech, merriment, and with the gladness of spiritual desire await holy Easter.

Let each one, however, make known to his Abbot what he

offereth and let it be done with his approval and blessing; because what is done without permission of the spiritual father will be imputed to presumption and vain glory, and not to merit. Therefore, let all be done with the approval of the Abbot.

50

OF BRETHREN WHO WORK A LONG DISTANCE FROM THE ORATORY OR ARE ON A JOURNEY

The brethren who are at work too far away, and cannot come to the oratory at the appointed time, and the Abbot hath assured himself that such is the case—let them perform the Work of God in the fear of God and on bended knees where they are working. In like manner let those who are sent on a journey not permit the appointed hours to pass by; but let them say the office by themselves as best they can, and not neglect to fulfil the obligation of divine service.

51

OF THE BRETHREN WHO DO NOT GO VERY FAR AWAY

A brother who is sent out on any business and is expected to return to the monastery the same day, may not presume to eat outside, even though he be urgently requested to do so, unless, indeed, it is commanded him by his Abbot. If he act otherwise, let him be excommunicated.

52

OF THE ORATORY OF THE MONASTERY

Let the oratory be what it is called, and let nothing else be done or stored there. When the Work of God is finished, let all go out with the deepest silence, and let reverence be shown to God; that a brother who perhaps desireth to pray especially by himself is not prevented by another's misconduct. But if perhaps another desireth to pray alone in private, let him enter with simplicity and pray, not with a loud voice, but with tears and fervor of heart. Therefore, let him who doth not say his prayers in this way, not be permitted to stay in the oratory after the Work of God is finished, as we said, that another may not be disturbed.

53

OF THE RECEPTION OF GUESTS

Let all guests who arrive be received as Christ, because He will say: "I was a stranger and you took Me in" (Mt 25:35). And let due honor be shown to all, especially to those "of the household of the faith" (Gal 6:10) and to wayfarers.

When, therefore, a guest is announced, let him be met by the Superior and the brethren with every mark of charity. And let them first pray together, and then let them associate with one another in peace. This kiss of peace should not be given before a prayer hath first been said, on account of satanic deception. In the greeting let all humility be shown to the guests, whether coming or going; with the head bowed down or the whole body prostrate on the ground, let Christ be adored in them as He is also received.

When the guests have been received, let them be accompanied to prayer, and after that let the Superior, or whom he shall bid, sit down with them. Let the divine law be read to the guest that he may be edified, after which let every kindness be shown him. Let the fast be broken by the Superior in deference to the guest, unless, perchance, it be a day of solemn fast, which cannot be broken. Let the brethren, however, keep the customary fast. Let the Abbot pour the water on the guest's hands, and let both the Abbot and the whole brotherhood wash the feet of all the guests. When they have been washed, let them say this verse: "We have received Thy mercy, O God, in the midst of Thy temple" (Ps 47[48]:10). Let the greatest care be taken, especially in the reception of the poor and travelers, because Christ is received more specially in them; whereas regard for the wealthy itself procureth them respect.

Let the kitchen of the Abbot and the guests be apart, that the brethren may not be disturbed by the guests who arrive at uncertain times and who are never wanting in the monastery. Let two brothers who are able to fulfil this office well go into the kitchen for a year. Let help be given them as they need it, that they may serve without murmuring; and when they have not enough to do, let them go out again for work where it is commanded them. Let this course be followed, not only in this office, but in all the offices of the monastery—that whenever the brethren need help, it be given them, and that when they have nothing to do, they again obey orders. Moreover, let also a God-fearing brother have assigned to him the apartment of the guests, where there should be sufficient number of beds made up; and let the house of God be wisely managed by the wise.

On no account let anyone who is not ordered to do so, associate or speak with guests; but if he meet or see them, having saluted them humbly, as we have said, and asked a blessing, let him pass on saying that he is not allowed to speak with a guest.

54

WHETHER A MONK SHOULD RECEIVE LETTERS OR ANYTHING ELSE

Let it not be allowed at all for a monk to give or to receive letters, tokens, or gifts of any kind, either from parents or any other person, nor from each other, without the permission of the Abbot. But even if anything is sent him by his parents, let him not presume to accept it before it hath been make known to the Abbot. And if he order it to be accepted, let it be in the Abbot's power to give it to whom he pleaseth. And let not the brother to whom perchance it was sent, become sad, that "no chance be given to the devil" (Eph 4:27; 1 Tm 5:14). But whosoever shall presume to act otherwise, let him fall under the discipline of the Rule.

55

OF THE CLOTHING AND THE FOOTGEAR OF THE BRETHREN

Let clothing be given to the brethren according to the circumstances of the place and the nature of the climate in which they live, because in cold regions more is needed, while in warm regions less. This consideration, therefore, resteth with the Abbot. We believe, however, that for a temperate climate a cowl and a tunic for each monk are sufficient,—a woolen cowl for winter and a thin or worn one for summer, and a scapular for work, and stockings and shoes as covering for the feet. Let the monks not worry about the color or the texture of all these things, but let them be such as can be bought more cheaply. Let the Abbot, however, look to the size, that these garments are not too small, but fitted for those who are to wear them.

Let those who receive new clothes always return the old ones, to be put away in the wardrobe for the poor. For it is sufficient for a monk to have two tunics and two cowls, for wearing at night and for washing. Hence, what is over and above is superfluous and must be taken away. So, too, let them return stockings and whatever is old, when they receive anything new. Let those who are sent out on a journey receive trousers from the wardrobe, which, on their return, they will replace there, washed. The cowls and the tunics should also be a little better than the ones they usually wear, which they received from the wardrobe when they set out on a journey, and give back when they return.

For their bedding, let a straw mattress, a blanket, a coverlet, and a pillow be sufficient. These beds must, however, be frequently examined by the Abbot, to prevent personal goods from being found. And if anything should be found with anyone that he did not receive from the Abbot, let him fall under the severest discipline. And that this vice of private ownership may be cut off by the root, let everything necessary be given by the Abbot; namely, cowl, tunic, stockings, shoes, girdle, knife, pen, needle, towel, writing tablet; that all pretence of want may be removed. In this connection, however, let the following sentence from the Acts of the Apostles always be kept in mind by the Abbot: "And distribution was made to every man according as he had need" (Acts 4:35). In this manner, therefore, let the Abbot also have regard for the infirmities of the needy, not for the bad will of the envious. Yet in all his decisions, let the Abbot think of God's retribution.

56
OF THE ABBOT'S TABLE

Let the Abbot's table always be with the guests and travelers. When, however, there are no guests, let it be in his power to invite any of the brethren he desireth. Let him provide, however, that one or two of the seniors always remain with the brethren for the sake of discipline.

57

OF THE ARTISTS OF THE MONASTERY

If there be skilled workmen in the monastery, let them work at their art in all humility, if the Abbot giveth his permission. But if anyone of them should grow proud by reason of his art, in that he seemeth to confer a benefit on the monastery, let him be removed from that work and not return to it, unless after he hath humbled himself, the Abbot again ordereth him to do so. But if any of the work of the artists is to be sold, let them, through whose hands the transaction must pass, see to it, that they do not presume to practice any fraud on the monastery. Let them always be mindful of Ananias and Saphira, lest, perhaps, the death which these suffered in the body (cf Acts 5:1-11), they and all who practice any fraud in things belonging to the monastery suffer in the soul. On the other hand, as regards the prices of these things, let not the vice of avarice creep in, but let it always be given a little cheaper than it can be given by seculars, *That God May Be Glorified in All Things* (1 Pt 4:11).

58
OF THE MANNER OF ADMITTING BRETHREN

Let easy admission not be given to one who newly cometh to change his life; but, as the Apostle saith, "Try the spirits, whether they be of God" (1 Jn 4:1). If, therefore, the newcomer keepeth on knocking, and after four or five days it is seen that he patiently beareth the harsh treatment offered him and the difficulty of admission, and that he persevereth in his request, let admission be granted him, and let him live for a few days in the apartment of the guests.

But afterward let him live in the apartment of novices, and there let him meditate, eat, and sleep. Let a senior also be appointed for him, who is qualified to win souls, who will observe him with great care and see whether he really seeketh God, whether he is eager for the Work of God, obedience and humiliations. Let him be shown all the hard and rugged things through which we pass on to God.

If he promiseth to remain steadfast, let this Rule be read to him in order after the lapse of two months, and let it be said to him: Behold the law under which thou desirest to combat. If thou canst keep it, enter; if, however, thou canst not, depart freely. If he still persevereth, then let him be taken back to the aforesaid apartment of the novices, and let him be tried again in all patience. And after the lapse of six months let the Rule be read over to him, that he may know for what purpose he entereth. And if he still remaineth firm, let the same Rule be read to him again after four months. And if, after having weighed the matter with himself he promiseth to keep everything, and to do everything that is commanded him, then let him be received into the community, knowing that he is now placed under the law of the Rule, and that from that day forward it is no longer permitted to him to wrest his neck from under the yoke of the Rule, which after so long a deliberation he was at liberty either to refuse or to accept.

Let him who is received promise in the oratory, in the presence of all, before God and His saints, stability, the conversion of morals, and obedience, in order that, if he should ever do otherwise, he may know that he will be condemned by God "Whom he mocketh." Let him make a written statement of his promise in the name of the saints whose relics are there, and of the Abbot there present. Let him write this document with his own hand; or at least, if he doth not know how to write, let another write it at his request, and let the novice make his mark, and with his own hand place it on the altar. When he hath placed it there, let the novice next begin the verse: "Uphold me, O Lord, according to Thy word and I shall live; and let me not be confounded in my expectations" (Ps 118[119]:116). Then let all the brotherhood repeat this verse three times, adding the *Gloria Patri*.

The let that novice brother cast himself down at the feet of all, that they may pray for him; and from that day let him be counted in the brotherhood. If he hath any property, let him first either dispose of it to the poor or bestow it on the monastery by a formal donation, reserving nothing for himself as indeed he should know that from that day onward he will no longer have power even over his own body.

Let him, therefore, be divested at once in the oratory of the garments with which he is clothed, and be vested in the garb of the monastery. But let the clothes of which he was divested by laid by in the wardrobe to be preserved, that, if on the devil's suasion he should ever consent to leave the monastery (which God forbid) he be then stripped of his monastic habit and cast out. But let him not receive the document of his profession which the Abbot took from the altar, but let it be preserved in the monastery.

59

OF THE CHILDREN OF THE NOBLE AND OF THE POOR WHO ARE OFFERED

If it happen that a nobleman offereth his son to God in the monastery and the boy is of tender age, let his parents execute the written promise which we have mentioned above; and with the oblation let them wrap that document and the boy's hand in the altar cloth and thus offer him.

As to their property, let them bind themselves under oath in the same document that they will never give him anything themselves nor through any other person, nor in any way whatever, nor leave a chance for his owning anything; or else, if they refuse to do this and want to make an offering to the monastery as an alms for their own benefit, let them make a donation to the monastery of whatever goods they wish to give, reserving to themselves the income of it, if they so desire. And let everything be so barred that the boy remain in no uncertainty, which might deceive and ruin him (which God forbid)—a pass we have learned by experience.

Let those who are poor act in like manner. But as to those who have nothing at all, let them simply make the declaration, and with the oblation offer their son in the presence of witnesses.

60

OF PRIESTS WHO MAY WISH TO LIVE IN THE MONASTERY

If a priest asketh to be received into the monastery, let consent not be granted too readily; still, if he urgently persisteth in his request, let him know that he must keep the whole discipline of the Rule, and that nothing will be relaxed in his favor, that it may be as it is written: "Friend, whereunto art thou come" (Mt 26:25)?

It may be granted him, however, to stand next after the Abbot, and to give the blessing, or to celebrate Mass, but only if the Abbot ordereth him to do so; but if he doth not bid him, let him not presume to do anything under whatever consideration, knowing that he is under the discipline of the Rule, and let him rather give examples of humility to all. But if there is a question of an appointment in the monastery, or any other matter, let him be ranked by the time of his entry into the monastery, and not by the place granted him in consideration of the priesthood.

But if a cleric, moved by the same desire, wisheth to join the monastery, let him too have a middle place, provided he promiseth to keep the Rule and personal stability.

61

HOW STRANGER MONKS ARE TO BE RECEIVED

If a monk who is a stranger, arriveth from a distant place and desireth to live in the monastery as a guest, and is satisfied with the customs he findeth there, and doth not trouble the monastery with superfluous wants, but is satisfied with what he findeth, let him be received for as long a time as he desireth. Still, if he should reasonably, with humility and charity, censure or point out anything, let the Abbot consider discreetly whether the Lord did not perhaps send him for that very purpose. If later on he desireth to declare his stability let his wish not be denied, and especially since his life could be known during his stay as a guest.

But if during the time that he was a guest he was found to be troublesome and disorderly, he must not only not associate with the monastic body but should even be politely requested to leave, that others may not be infected by his evil life. But if he hath not been such as deserveth to be cast forth, he should not only be admitted to join the brotherhood, if he apply, but he should even be urged to remain, that others may be taught by his example, because we serve one Lord and fight under one King everywhere. If the Abbot recognize him to be such a one he may also place him in a somewhat higher rank.

The Abbot may, however, place not only a monk, but also those of the aforesaid grades of priests and clerics, in a higher place than that of their entry, if he seeth their lives to be such as to deserve it. But let the Abbot take care never to admit a monk of any other known monastery to residence, without the consent of his Abbot or commendatory letters, because it is written: "What thou wilt not have done to thyself, do not to another" (Tb 4:16).

62

OF THE PRIESTS OF THE MONASTERY

If the Abbot desireth to have a priest or a deacon ordained, let him select from among his monks one who is worthy to discharge the priestly office.

But let the one who hath been ordained be on his guard against arrogance and pride, and let him not attempt to do anything but what is commanded him by the Abbot, knowing that he is now all the more subject to the discipline of the Rule; and in consequence of the priesthood let him not forget the obedience and discipline of the Rule, but advance more and more in godliness.

Let him, however, always keep the place which he had when he entered the monastery, except when he is engaged in sacred functions, unless the choice of the community and the wish of the Abbot have promoted him in acknowledgment of the merit of his life. Let him know, however, that he must observe the Rule prescribed by the Deans and the Superiors.

If he should otherwise, let him be judged, not as a priest, but as a rebel; and if after frequent warnings he doth not amend, and his guilt is clearly shown, let him be cast forth from the monastery, provided his obstinacy is such that he will neither submit nor obey the Rule.

63

OF THE ORDER IN THE MONASTERY

Let all keep their order in the monastery in such wise, that the time of their conversion and the merit of their life distinguish it, or as the Abbot hath directed. Let the Abbot not disorder the flock committed to him, nor by an arbitrary use of his power dispose of anything unjustly; but let him always bear in mind that he will have to give an account to God of all his judgments and works. Hence in the order that he hath established, or that the brethren had, let them approach for the kiss of peace, for Communion, intone the psalms, and stand in choir.

And in no place whatever let age determine the order or be a disadvantage; because Samuel and Daniel when mere boys judged the priests (cf 1 Sam. 3; Dan 13:44-62). Excepting those, therefore, whom, as we have said, the Abbot from higher motives hath advanced, or, for certain reasons, hath lowered, let all the rest take their place as they are converted: thus, for instance, let him who came into the monastery at the second hour of the day, know that he is younger than he who came at the first hour, whatever his age or dignity may be.

Children are to be kept under discipline at all times and by everyone. Therefore, let the younger honor their elders, and the older love the younger.

In naming each other let no one be allowed to address another by his simple name; but let the older style the younger brethren, brothers; let the younger, however, call their elders, fathers, by which is implied the reverence due to a father. But because the Abbot is believed to hold the place of Christ, let him be styled Lord and Abbot, not only by assumption on his part, but out of love and reverence for Christ. Let him think of this and so show himself, that he be worthy of such an honor. Wherever, then, the brethren meet each other, let the younger ask the blessing from the older; and when the older passeth by, let the younger rise and give him place to sit; and let the younger not presume to sit down with him unless his elder biddeth him to do so, that it may be done as it is written: "In honor preventing one another" (Rom 12:10).

Let children and boys take their places in the oratory and at table with all due discipline; outdoors, however, or wherever they may be, let them be under custody and discipline until they reach the age of understanding.

64

OF THE ELECTION OF THE ABBOT

In the election of an Abbot let this always be observed as a rule, that he be placed in the position whom the whole community with one consent, in the fear of God, or even a small part, with sounder judgment, shall elect. But let him who is to be elected be chosen for the merit of his life and the wisdom of his doctrine, though he be the last in the community.

But even if the whole community should by mutual consent elect a man who agreeth to connive at their evil ways (which God forbid) and these irregularities in some come to the knowledge of the Bishop to whose diocese the place belongeth, or to neighboring Abbots, or Christian people, let them not permit the intrigue of the wicked to succeed, but let them appoint a worthy steward over the house of God, knowing that they shall receive a bountiful reward for this action, if they do it with a pure intention and godly zeal; whereas, on the other hand, they commit a sin if they neglect it.

But when the Abbot hath been elected let him bear in mind

how great a burden he hath taken upon himself, and to whom he must give an account of his stewardship (cf Lk 16:2); and let him be convinced that it becometh him better to serve than to rule. He must, therefore, be versed in the divine law, that he may know whence "to bring forth new things and old" (Mt 13:52). Let him be chaste, sober, and merciful, and let him always exalt "mercy above judgment" (Jas 2:13), that he also may obtain mercy.

Let him hate vice, but love the brethren. And even in his corrections, let him act with prudence and not go to extremes, lest, while he aimeth to remove the rust too thoroughly, the vessel be broken. Let him always keep his own frailty in mind, and remember that "the bruised reed must not be broken" (Is 42:3). In this we are not saying that he should allow evils to take root, but that he cut them off with prudence and charity, as he shall see it is best for each one, as we have already said; and let him aim to be loved rather than feared.

Let him not be fussy or over-anxious, exacting, or headstrong; let him not be jealous or suspicious, because he will never have rest. In all his commands, whether they refer to things spiritual or temporal, let him be cautious and considerate. Let him be discerning and temperate in the tasks which he enjoineth, recalling the discretion of holy Jacob who saith: "If I should cause my flocks to be overdriven, they would all die in one day" (Gen 33:13). Keeping in view these and other dictates of discretion, the mother of virtues, let him so temper everything that the strong may still have something to desire and the weak may not draw back. Above all, let him take heed that he keep this Rule in all its detail; that when he hath served well he may hear from the Lord what the good servant heard who gave his fellow-servants bread in season: "Amen, I say to you," He saith,"he shall set him over all his goods" (Mt 24:47).

65

OF THE PRIOR OF THE MONASTERY

It often happeneth indeed, that grave scandals arise in monasteries out of the appointment of the Prior; since there are some who, puffed up with the wicked spirit of pride and thinking themselves to be second Abbots, set up a despotic rule, foster scandals, and excite quarrels in the community, and especially in those places where also the Prior is appointed by the same Bishop or the same Abbots who appointeth his Abbot. How foolish this is can easily be seen; because, from the very beginning of his appointment, matter for pride is furnished him, when his thoughts suggest to him that now he is exempt from the authority of the Abbot, because "thou too hast been appointed by those by whom the Abbot was appointed." From this source arise envy, discord, slander, quarrels, jealousy, and disorders. While the Abbot and the Prior are thus at variance with each other, it must follow that their souls are endangered by this discord and that those who are under them, as long as they humor the parties, go to ruin. The fault of this evil resteth on the heads of those who were the authors of such disorders.

We foresee, therefore, that for the preservation of peace and charity it is best that the government of the monastery should depend on the will of the Abbot; and if it can be done, let the affairs of the monastery (as we have explained before) be attended to by deans, as the Abbot shall dispose; so that, the same office being shared by many, no one may become proud.

If, however, the place require it, or the brotherhood reasonably and with humility make the request, and the Abbot shall deem it advisable, let the Abbot himself appoint as Prior whomever, with the advice of God-fearing brethren, he shall select. But let the Prior reverently do what his Abbot hath enjoined on him, doing nothing against the will or the direction of the Abbot; for the higher he is placed above others, the more careful should he be to obey the precepts of the Rule.

If the Prior be found disorderly or blinded by vainglory, or hath been proved to be a contemner of the Holy Rule, let him be admonished up to the fourth time; if he doth not amend, let the correction of the regular discipline be applied to him. But if he doth not amend even then, let him be deposed from the office of priorship, and another who is worthy be appointed in his stead. But if even afterward he be not quiet and submissive in the brotherhood, let him also be expelled from the monastery. Still, let the Abbot reflect that he must give an account to God for all his judgments, lest perhaps envy or jealousy should sear his conscience.

66

OF THE PORTER OF THE MONASTERY

Let a wise old man be placed at the door of the monastery, one who knoweth how to take and give an answer, and whose mature age doth not permit him to stray about.

The porter should have a cell near the door, that they who come may always find one present from whom they may obtain an answer. As soon as anyone knocketh or a poor person calleth, let him answer, "Thanks be to God," or invoke a blessing, and with the meekness of the fear of God let him return an answer speedily in the fervor of charity. If the porter hath need of assistance, let him have a younger brother.

If it can be done, the monastery should be so situated that all the necessaries, such as water, the mill, the garden, are enclosed, and the various arts may be plied inside of the monastery, so that there may be no need for the monks to go about outside, because it is not good for their souls. But we desire that this Rule be read quite often in the community, that none of the brethren may excuse himself of ignorance.

67

OF THE BRETHREN WHO ARE SENT ON A JOURNEY

Let the brethren who are to be sent on a journey recommend themselves to the prayers of all the brotherhood and of the Abbot. And after the last prayer at the Work of God, let a commemoration always be made for the absent brethren.

On the day that the brethren return from the journey, let them lie prostrate on the floor of the oratory at all the Canonical Hours, when the Work of God is finished, and ask the prayers of all on account of failings, for fear that the sight of evil or the sound of frivolous speech should have surprised them on the way.

And let no one presume to relate to another what he hath seen or heard outside of the monastery, because it is most hurtful. But if anyone presume to do so, let him undergo the penalty of the Rule. In like manner let him be punished who shall presume to go beyond the enclosure of the monastery, or anywhere else, or to do anything, however little, without the order of the Abbot.

68
IF A BROTHER IS COMMANDED TO DO IMPOSSIBLE THINGS

If, perchance, any difficult or impossible tasks be enjoined on a brother, let him nevertheless receive the order of him who commandeth with all meekness and obedience. If, however, he see that the gravity of the task is altogether beyond his strength, let him quietly and seasonably submit the reasons for his inability to his Superior, without pride, protest, or dissent. If, however, after his explanation the Superior still insisteth on his command, let the younger be convinced that so it is good for him; and let him obey from love, relying on the help of God.

69

THAT IN THE MONASTERY NO ONE PRESUME TO DEFEND ANOTHER

Care must be taken that on no occasion one monk try to defend another in the monastery, or to take his part, even though they be closely related by ties of blood. Let it not be attempted by the monks in any way; because such conduct may give rise to very grave scandal. If anyone overstep this rule, let him be severely punished.

70

THAT NO ONE PRESUME TO STRIKE ANOTHER

Let every occasion for presumption be avoided in the monastery. We decree that no one be permitted to excommunicate or to strike any one of his brethren, unless the Abbot hath given him the authority. But let those who transgress be taken to task in the presence of all, that the others may fear (cf 1 Tm 5:20).

Let all, however, exercise diligent and watchful care over the discipline of children, until the age of fifteen; but even that, within due limits and with discretion. For if anyone should presume to chastise those of more advanced years, without the command of the Abbot, or should be unduly provoked with children, let him be subject to the discipline of the Rule; because it is written: "What thou dost not wish to be done to thee, do not thou to another" (Tb 4:16).

71

THAT THE BRETHREN BE OBEDIENT TO ONE ANOTHER

The brethren must render the service of obedience not only to the Abbot, but they must thus also obey one another, knowing that they shall go to God by this path of obedience. Hence, granted the command of the Abbot and of the Superiors who are appointed by him (to which we do not permit private commands to be preferred), in other respects let the younger brethren obey their elders with all charity and zeal. But if anyone is found to be obstinate, let him be punished.

And if a brother be punished in any way by the Abbot or by any of his Superiors for even a slight reason or if he perceive that the temper of any of his Superiors is but slightly ruffled or excited against him in the least, let him without delay cast himself down on the ground at his feet making satisfaction, until the agitation is quieted by a blessing. If anyone scorn to do this, either let him undergo corporal punishment, or, if he be obstinate, let him be expelled from the monastery.

72

OF THE VIRTUOUS ZEAL WHICH THE MONKS OUGHT TO HAVE

As there is a harsh and evil zeal which separateth from God and leadeth to hell, so there is a virtuous zeal which separateth from vice and leadeth to God and life everlasting.

Let the monks, therefore, practice this zeal with most ardent love; namely, that in honor they forerun one another (cf Rom 12:10). Let them bear their infirmities, whether of body or mind, with the utmost patience; let them vie with one another in obedience. Let no one follow what he thinketh useful to himself, but rather to another. Let them practice fraternal charity with a chaste love.

Let them fear God and love their Abbot with sincere and humble affection; let them prefer nothing whatever to Christ, and may He lead us all together to life everlasting.

73

OF THIS, THAT NOT THE WHOLE OBSERVANCE OF RIGHTEOUSNESS IS LAID DOWN IN THIS RULE

Now, we have written this Rule that, observing it in monasteries, we may show that we have acquired at least some moral righteousness, or a beginning of the monastic life.

On the other hand, he that hasteneth on to the perfection of the religious life, hath at hand the teachings of the holy Fathers, the observance of which leadeth a man to the height of perfection. For what page or what utterance of the divinely inspired books of the Old and the New Testament is not a most exact rule of human life? Or, what book of the holy Catholic Fathers doth not loudly proclaim how we may go straight to our Creator? So, too, the collations of the Fathers, and their institutes and lives, and the rule of our holy Father, Basil—what are they but the monuments of the virtues of exemplary and obedient monks? But for us slothful, disedifying, and negligent monks they are a source for shame and confusion.

Thou, therefore, who hastenest to the heavenly home, with the help of Christ fulfil this least rule written for a beginning; and then thou shalt with God's help attain at last to the greater heights of knowledge and virtue which we have mentioned above.

Copyright © 2020 by FV Éditions
Cover picture : *Saint Benoît de Nursie* by Alessandro Turchi.
Ebook ISBN : 979-10-299-0905-4
Paperback ISBN : 9798644892129
Hardcover ISBN : 979-10-299-0906-1
All rights reserved.

Also Available

THE DIDACHE

www.ingramcontent.com/pod-product-compliance
Lightning Source LLC
LaVergne TN
LVHW042248070526
838201LV00089B/72